Expounding the Doubtful Points

Wing Tek Lum

Bamboo Ridge Press
1987

This is a special double issue of *Bamboo Ridge, The Hawaii Writers' Quarterly,* issues no. 34 and 35, Summer and Fall 1987, ISSN 0733-0308.

ISBN 0-910043-14-0
Library of Congress Catalog Card Number: 87-72145
Indexed in the American Humanities Index
Copyright 1987 Wing Tek Lum
Published by Bamboo Ridge Press.

The cover was designed by Doug Young, using a section of his watercolor painting, "One Thirty-five." *Amerasia Journal, The American Pen, Bamboo Ridge, Bridge, Bulletin of Concerned Asian Scholars, Chelsea, Contact II, East/West, Hapa, Hawaii Review, Mana, Missouri Review, New York Quarterly, The Paper, Poetry Hawaii, Talk Story,* and *Yardbird Reader* first published several of these poems. "To the Old Masters" originally appeared in *Poetry.* "I Caught Him Once" and "Going Bananas" were also dramatized in *Island Slices,* a 1984 production of Honolulu Theatre for Youth. Mahalo to all.

Bamboo Ridge Press is a non-profit, tax exempt organization formed to foster the appreciation, understanding, and creation of literary, visual, audio-visual and performing arts by and about Hawaii's people. Your tax-deductible contributions are welcomed.

Bamboo Ridge, The Hawaii Writers' Quarterly is supported in part by grants from the State Foundation on Culture and the Arts (SFCA). The SFCA is is funded by appropriations from the Hawaii State Legislature and by grants from the National Endowment for the Arts.

Subscriptions to *Bamboo Ridge, The Hawaii Writers' Quarterly* are available for $12 per year.

Editors: Eric Chock and Darrell H.Y. Lum
Managing editor: Mavis Hara
Typesetting: Kailua Quick Print
Production: Sun, an educational communications co.
Printing: Thomson-Shore, Inc.

Bamboo Ridge Press
P.O. Box 61781
Honolulu, Hawaii 96822-8781

for T'ao Ch'ien, for Frank Chin

Table of Contents

Part One

What I Want

All I need
is a long table, smooth
and level, laminated
if possible, and sturdy
enough to type on.

I like
a lot of lights,
the directional kind
that I can swivel
around, the kind
that go PING at the flick
of my finger.

I need
a bed, too, and use
of an icebox
perhaps, where I can store
juice and tangerines
and the yogurt mixed
by myself, ready
to eat in the mornings.

I want
a place where I don't
have to put
on my pants to go
piss, where I can scratch
my ass whenever I want to,
and take a shower
everyday without
feeling guilty about
monopolizing the hot water
or the bathroom time.

I would like

to stay up at all
hours of the night, wander
barefoot about,
maybe read some
book, or else listen
to the trucks going by,
and to the radiators'
clank,
          while I wait,
unshaven, without you.

To a Poet Who Says He's Stopped Writing (Temporarily)

I don't care what you do for a living
sell stocks or bonds or both
drive a cab full time
wait on tables
        at that new jazz spot in Waikiki

I don't care what grand thoughts have moved you
the good image of your grandmother's smile
your delights at eating meatless meals
or that burning desire
        to let every child speak a language of his own

There have been the times
when those wishful sentiments aren't enough
when you must lay aside all other claims on your life
simply to satisfy
        that single all-consuming craving

And now you are waiting
not merely driving home at night with the radio off
or washing your hair in the shower
or lying in bed, face down,
        your lights out and the shades drawn

These periods are as essential
as that moment you sit down in a rush
your favorite pen in hand
pulling out that journal
        you've always carried for this very purpose

And when the point scratches surface
flesh is made word
and these small truths of your existence
illumine the page
        like laser light, scorching our hearts forever

To a Classmate Just Dead

"When we last clasped hands before the gate
I did not think that you would go ahead."
—T'ao Ch'ien

My two-year-old thinks it's neat
to pick up pebbles off the walk
following, as we did, your father's custom
placing them atop the small concrete block
set to one side
by the flat, dirt-covered ground
serving as your temporary marker.

It's more for the living, he explains,
to let any passerby know
that someone else was here.

It's as if deep down
we all agree that you are dead
and cannot see these pebbles here,
cannot smell the rose that I have left,
much less hear my silent prayer to you.

And that's the problem.
Our visit, like this poem,
has been more for the living,
no longer your concern
and one day no longer ours.

To Li Po

I liked that poem
—the one about getting drunk,
three hundred gold cups of wine,
to drown away the sorrows
of generations.
                    In those days
for every poem you wrote
a million Chinamen suffered to die.

     pen from bone
     brush from hair
     ink from blood

They were illiterate, you knew.
Better than words,
the liquor was solace enough for them.

Part Two

But It Was

We were in the old house in the kitchen.
I was sitting at the dining table
and they were cooking by the stoves.

And somehow it was me, the cupid,
who reminded them
that it was their anniversary.

And he uttered a surprise
and embraced her
with a smooch right on her lips.

And she pushed him away
flustered and complaining about his stubble
and how this was no big deal.

But it was.
It was the only time
I ever did see them kiss.

My Mother Really Knew

My father was a tough cookie,
his friends still tell me with a smile.
He was hot-tempered
and had to have his own way,
but they loved him nonetheless,
and so did I.

I remember that
for maybe the first decade of my life
I had to kiss him every night
before I went to bed.

There was one time
he got into a big argument
with the rest of us at dinnertime,
and afterwards when he was in his study
I had to go to sleep
and refused to see him,
a chip off the old block.

But my mother and elder brothers
coaxed me to his door,
and I ran in
and pecked his cheek
without saying a word,
and went to bed
thinking of how unfair life was.

Love, my mother really knew,
was like these islands
formed in part
by tidal waves and hurricanes
and the eruptions of volcanoes,
which suddenly appear
and just as suddenly go away.

She Made Quite Sure of That

A flabby mound,
its nipple squat at the top
—that was the left breast.
The right side was more interesting:
her ribs like bald ridges
protruding from underneath
that patch of thigh stretched thin
so smooth and shiny
flesh cauterized to heal on tight.
I remember both of us
were on her bed,
her blouse was open
(I guess no padded bra that day).
I was so serious about her luck;
if it had happened on her left
her heart might have been wounded too.
She must have smiled then,
this straight-laced woman.
I was a happy child
—she made quite sure of that—
not from an innocence
of all mothers' chests being just like hers,
rather out of gratitude that
as if with one less layer
she revealed more of herself to me.

I Watched a Quiet Lady

At the age of sixteen, I watched a quiet lady,
dying. Her jaundiced body was shrivelled
against bright, hospital-clean sheets. Only
her belly was full-bloated, bursting of a malignancy
that would soon blunt her fears. Determined, I followed
her once steady eyes, floating uncontrolled and white,
listening to the thin, clawing gasps of breath
that finally evaporated within the hollow gap
formed by her lips.
                    Later, as I gathered together
her robe, her flowers, and her comb, I chanced
to gaze upon this corpse, helpless, lying
in its solemn air of calm. There seemed no longer
a lady, who once bore me in a girlhood cancer.
The silent skin enshrouded no being, no agony,
no joy. Clutching the guard rail beside the bed,
I wondered what else could there be left for me to do.

I Did Not Understand

She was lying on the bed.
We were packing up
her belongings in a suitcase.
The surgeon arrived—
he was a long-time friend
—to wish us his condolences.
We conversed for a while
on how things had changed
so drastically within that week,
on what she last told us
the day before. About to go,
we shook hands all around.
My father ended with something
in Chinese: a short
appropriate sentence or two
—perhaps an old proverb,
or even that silly platitude
that *this* is the way it is.
I had hoped he would.
I did not understand a word,
but it moved me deeply.

The Door Was Opened

The family store always kept its door open
even after air conditioning was installed.

One day the mother died
and her men argued throughout the night.

Business as usual is what she would want
the father said.

Her sons replied
she lived for more than just the store.

The next morning, as a compromise,
the door was opened, but less than halfway

—what with the lilies hung outside
only a child could slip through sideways.

Twenty Two Years

A half-smoked cigarette
discarded in an ashtray
slowly burning still

forming a cylinder of ashes
flecked with grays and white
so roundly molded

that I am tempted
to touch it
to confirm its perfection

but I do not
content to accept
what remains

as I have done
for twenty two years
with my memories of you.

A Picture of My Mother's Family

At a summer home in Ningpo, near Shanghai,
your family (circa 1915) poses on the stone floor entryway
between the rise of steps and the wood front door.
Four girls are spread about the parents,
who are seated. All are in warm clothing,
finely dressed. It is perhaps morning, the coolness
captured now in such clear light: they seem, somehow,
more illumined by beams emanating from the moon.

On the right, Ming, the second-born, my living aunt,
has on a dark wool dress and brocaded top of silk
that does not cover her sleeves. She tiptoes slightly,
for she leans to one side on her hidden right arm
bracing, it would seem, on the edge of her father's chair.
Her face — cocked to her right in front of his chest —
is plump. The supple mouth I recognize
smiles downward, frowning: sad and shy
in her own young world. This photograph is hers;
last year she gave it to me in remembrance of you.

My grandfather is seated on white upholstery,
upright, balding and in black, even to his bow tie.
The shine on his shoes reflects into the camera
as he looks on, disregarding the cluster of children,
towards his right faraway. I imagine a dark rose
has caught his proud eye, though I do not know
if such flowers have ever grown there.
The grain of the picture reveals his fine hands,
as if all were focused upon them alone.
The fingers are brown and slender, recalling
that he was a doctor, and that these are doctor's hands.
Gnarled roots, they had grown as pale as his beard
and clothes, when we saw him — I at the age of five
in Hong Kong, after he was allowed in for the last time.

Holding his right hand in her small clasp,

her arm snuggled against his thigh, the third daughter
(maybe three) glances with eyebrows raised
somewhere in the direction of her father's gaze.
Her stance is as wide as her padded skirt, disclosing
beneath a small foot balancing on its outer side.
I guess that her silk top is red, a color
of wide cherries. The shortest in the picture,
she stands dwarfed by the shadows looming behind her.
Funny, but I don't even know her name; I think
she was the one, you said, who never reached her teens.

Lucy, the youngest sister, leans forward
on her mother's lap: squirming, I assume,
for her left arm is in a blur, swinging,
her mouth opened round, voicing her discomfort.
She is all white in a doll's bonnet and long dress,
as if she were attending her own wedding.
More likely, it's her birthday...
She never married, moved to Chicago near Ming.
At forty, she visited our home, skinny and sallow
from cancer. Soon after, picking me up
from school, you told me, "she just passed away."

Caught at that moment, your mother looks into the lens,
while restraining her daughter: her hands in front
encircling the waist. She wears a wan smile,
almost serene. Partly it's because of her face,
which seems flat. I can discern no part of her nose,
except for the line of a shadow beneath her nostrils.
Her trousers are nearly covered by the spread
of Lucy's dress. I notice that wrinkles have begun
to set under her eyes; they make her appear
out of focus, like crying. I muse about
whether her feet were bound. A pastor's daughter,
she died young. My grandfather remarried.

The one on the left end, you are as tall
as your parents are when seated. With black boots on
you balance playfully on the balls of your feet,
a bit pigeon-toed. For you, the oldest,
your mother has combed all your hair back tightly
about your head; you wear to one side a paper flower:
white, to match your own long blouse and pants.
Although proper, I suppose, the sleeves
and the trouser legs are cut three-quarters length,
as if you had already outgrown these clothes.
Forearms exposed, I can see a thin bracelet
around each wrist. With your flat nose
and flower, I almost think you are a small clown.
Your mouth closed, you keep smiling straight at me.

To My Father

In our store that day
they gathered together
my grandfather among them
each in his turn
to cut off their queues:
the end of subservience.
They could have returned
the Republic just established
or, on the safe side,
waited a year
to grow back that braid.
No matter, they stayed.
Your father was young
and shrewd: the store flourished,
then the crops, the lands.

Out of your share
you sent us to the best schools;
we were to follow the dynasty
set by the Old Man.
But he had died
before I was born, his grave
all I could pay homage to.
I was freed from those old ways.
Today, unbraided,
my hair has grown long
because and in spite of those haircuts
you and he took.

So Proud: Dying with My Father

So proud to be yellow—
no matter that others revile

the color of plucked chicken
—you know our source

is the sun, the glitter of topaz,
of ripe pomelo and corn.

It is just:
your eyes, living symbol,

shine golden, revealing your true glory,
to the end,

liver rotting,
the bile nowhere else to go.

I Caught Him Once

Gruff old fut
never showed it
even after Ma died
even near his own end
stomach mostly gone
except one time
I caught him
in his room
talking to his nurse
wistful
"I don't know how much longer..."
him just sitting there
face so pale
not moving
the nurse standing at his back
leaning over
expertly
to wipe the tears
as they welled up

This Intimacy

It wasn't that hard
—him lying on his side
knees slightly bent
the hole between the large pale haunches.

"Are you ready?" I asked
more to me than him.

The nozzle went in,
I squeezed the tube
like a toothpaste roll
and waited.

"Okay, all pau,"
I had to say
and walked him to the bathroom.

I was the right one
for him to ask
though had there been a nurse
it would have been much better
all around.

Father and son,
so linked by years of love
and filial dislike
now sharing this intimacy:
my shame of his,
                        his shame of mine.

A Relief Overcame Me

After months of living at home
back in my old room

all of us taking shifts
listening to his snores

feeding him rich soups
and leading him to the bathroom

it did not occur to me
exactly when he would go

even after my second brother
and his family flew back

even after that one long night
we gathered around his bed

holding hands in a circle
calling out to him in turn

that the thirteen of us were there
as if that would stir him

from his fitful sleep.
It was not up to him or us.

That week my wife and I
broke off our wait to nap

because it seemed likely
that he would rest that way

for a while longer.
And somehow he died.

As I stood by his side
holding his lifeless hand in mine

a relief overcame me
immediate and unexpected.

We had shared with him his dying
and all of a sudden

that was for us
                    now over.

Privy to It All

"Inquiring of old friends
we learn half are ghosts."
—Tu Fu

In the first pew on the left
Aunty wears a navy blue suit
standing in front of Peter and his wife.
And as my turn comes to walk up to her
I get a little scared and self-conscious
thinking that she may forget who I am
with all these people watching.
But just as I say my name
she breaks out into a smile
and calls me "Wingy" like before.

And suddenly I feel so small
just like when she and Uncle
and the rest of the old Gang
used to come over to our home for dinners.
And what flashes through my mind
are all of those times together
when they were so alive and in their primes
sitting around those big, round tables,
discussing the front page news,
trading wisecracks and the latest gossip,
and sharing out loud their dreams.
They let down their hair
about their children and their businesses,
and at age ten I alone among my peers
was privy to it all.

We are like family,
Aunty reassures me as we clasp hands.
And as I take my seat
a sense of sadness comes over me,
looking about this church

filled now with family and friends
—and yet so few of those
from that group, from those years,
half incapacitated or dead
like my parents, and like these memories,
recalled now so infrequently
but for occasions such as this,
the farewells of a generation,
as I grow steadily older.

It's Something Our Family Has Always Done

On every trip away from these islands
on the day of departure and on the day of return
we go to the graves, all seven of them,
but for one the sum total of all of our ancestors
who died in this place we call home.

The drive to the cemetery is only five minutes long.
Stopping by a florist adds maybe ten minutes more.
Yet my wife and I on the day of our flight
are so rushed with packing and last minute chores.
Why do we still make the time to go?

The concrete road is one lane wide.
We turn around at the circle up at the top,
always to park just to the side of the large banyan tree
as the road begins its slope back down.
I turn the wheels; we now lock our car.

As if by rote, we bring anthuriums,
at least two flowers for each of our dead.
On our way we stop to pay our respects to the "Old Man"
—that first one lain here, all wind and water before him—
who watches over this graveyard, and our island home.

Approaching my grandparents, we divide up our offering,
placing their long stems into the holes filled with sand.
Squatting in front of each marble tablet,
I make it a point to read off their names in Chinese.
My hands pull out crabgrass running over stone.

I stand erect, clutching palm around fist,
swinging the air three times up and down.
My wife from the waist bows once, arms at her sides.
I manage to whisper a few phrases out loud,
conversing like my father would, as if all could hear.

We do Grandfather, Grandmother, and my parents below them.
Following the same path we always take,
we make our way through the tombstones and mounds,
skirting their concrete borders, to the other two Lums
and to our Granduncle on the Chang side.

Back up the hill, we spend a few moments by the curb
picking off black, thin burrs from our cuffs and socks.
We talk about what errands we must do next.
I glance around us at these man-made gardens,
thrust upon a slope of earth, spirit houses rising to the sky.

As I get into our car, and look out at the sea,
I am struck with the same thought as always.
We spend so little time in front of these graves
asking each in turn to protect us when we are far away.
I question them all: what good does it really do?

I have read ancient poets who parted with sorrow
from family and friends, fearing never to return.
Our oral histories celebrate brave peasants
daring oceans and the lonely beds: they looked even more
to blessings at long distance from their spirit dead.

My father, superstitious, even to the jet age,
still averred: but every little bit helps.
These sentiments I know, but I confess I do not feel.
Maybe it's for this loss that I still come here.
They are family, and I respect them so.

The Poet Imagines
His Grandfather's Thoughts on the Day He Died

This is the first year
the Dragon Eyes tree has ever borne fruit:
let us see what this omen brings.
Atop one of its exposed roots
a small frog squats, not moving, not even blinking.
I remember when my children were young
and this whole front yard was a taro patch:
we would take them out at night with a lantern
blinding the frogs just long enough
to sneak a hook up under the belly.
In those days we grew taro
as far as the eye could see;
I even invented a new kind of trough
lined inside with a wire mesh
so we could peel the skins with ease.
The King bought our poi,
and gave me a pounder one day.
It is made of stone,
and looks like the clapper of a bell, smooth and heavy.
I keep it in my bedroom now—there—on the dresser.
The fish we call Big Eyes
lies on an oval plate beside it.
I have not been hungry today.
The full bowl of rice attracts a fly
buzzing in anticipation.
I hear the laughter of one of my grandchildren
from the next room: which one is it?
Maybe someday one of them will think of me
and see the rainbows that I have seen,
the opium den in Annam that frightened me so,
my mother's tears when I left home.

Dear ancestors, all this is still one in my mind.

The Greatest Show on Earth

> "The ancients grudged even an inch of time"
> —T'ao Ch'ien

She floats, in black and white,
on her back
as if without gravity
legs bent and in small motion
little toes defined
one hand clenched in a fist
her head so large, out of proportion,
a mouth yawning.
The nurse points out to us
the spot pulsing on the screen
tiny dots all a-flurry:
a heart beats life.

This separate creature
transported from inside my wife
by sonic waves we cannot hear
onto this cathode screen
to give the performance of her life
and ours—
I feel no surge of pride
that she has sprung from my loins
in a commotion of our love
one night, conjoined,
an alchemy of fumbled masturbations
so difficult to fathom
so miraculous to confess
that we must doubt her perfection
as by God's will
that she will live
more mortal than ourselves.

The needle is withdrawn;
fluids that have cushioned her

will now be nurtured
for our selfish test
to learn which fickle choice
her true Creator has decreed.
Then we play God:
she lives or dies.

What if a lullaby is sung
out of tune?
Is it not better
than no song at all?
Our very presence in this room
this very privilege for us
for the first time
to see her
as she is
born into our eager eyes
is solely as a result
of one muted purpose.
No use to test
our doctor said
unless you will choose death.

There are as always
these solemn hymns:
that dread that
cradled in Fate's aimless arms
even our full lives mean nothing
the sorrow that it is really we
who have been put to test
our shame
that what we contemplate
compounds this inhumanity.
I know these solitudes well
and yet, today,
am moved by another passion

raw and delicate
the grand wonder of it all:
our daughter kicks
and turns her head
her body twists and arches
oblivious to her father's poetries.
I take it back;
there must be more.
This little heart beats stoutly
— if not a soul
a will to live.

Back home
we talk of nothing but
whose nose she has
the measurements of her head
how we forgot
to ask for a polaroid
in that excitement.
After seventeen weeks
of this mystery swelling
our hopes are at long last
so tangibly confirmed.
She is our gift no matter what
and she is here
now entering into our dreams
like no other
shaping our destinies, intertwined,
for better or for worse.
What ever happens to her now
we will never be alone again.

Flash

10-13-81
10:06 a.m.
a girl
6 lbs., 1 oz.
no name yet
all are well
parents
coping with
promotion
besides feedings
crying
diaper changes
baby
has smiled

That Extra Effort

Ching Jen at two months

Baby's fed and changed and tucked back in.
And the city outside our window is still dark
because it's only 4:30 in the morning
and I'm very tired and heavy under the eyes.
So I take off my clothes
and quickly slip back into bed
as it's one of the coldest nights of the year.
And as I lie on my back I hear from her crib
the squirming about under her covers
and that low cough-like whimper of her cry.
And I keep still, with my eyes closed,
hoping that she will conveniently fall asleep
as I'm lazy enough to catnap
and let her fuss a while longer.
And she is silent for a time
and as I listen I imagine
that her blanket now has covered up her face
or that she's vomited milk about her bed
or that a big bubble is still trapped inside her.
And instead of waiting any more I pull myself up
in a sudden surge that surprises even me.
I am beside her in an instant
and in that dim light see that she's all right,
her eyes shut, her cheeks fat and relaxed,
the tongue behind that part in her lips
sucking on a wholesome bottle of her dreams.
And then I pat her, and return to bed
thinking of what I just did, that extra effort,
which I would have never done before
—before I had a daughter whom I would care about so.

Going Bananas

Ching Jen at three months

It can occur
when you least expect
like after changing her diaper
for the 200th time
or after a feeding
or when you're coaxing her
to sleep in her crib
and she watches you
with her round dark eyes
her hair like a born comedian's
sticking out all over
her smooth relaxed cheeks
reminiscent of ivory
and all of a sudden
she breaks out
into a wide grin
toothless gums exposed
her eyes nearly shut
shaking her head
from side to side
so excitedly
going bananas over you.

To Live and Let Live

"...the tree of life also in the midst of the garden,
and the tree of the knowledge of good and evil."
—Genesis 2.9

We live on the side of a mountain, an old volcano in fact,
and all manner of insects pass through our condo
as we're on a low floor
and have never bothered to install screens to our windows.
Usually it's a moth or mosquito or a honeybee lost in the night.
In the summer there are also termites that rise as we dine.
Some of these bugs I have never seen before
like those lanky brown beetles
and that bright green one with a hard shell
I would have thought to find only in a museum.
The larger ones with stings I shoo away with my broom.
I will not hesitate to swat a fat roach.
But these are the exceptions.
Most others we have simply taken note of and ignored.
It's only been after the birth of our daughter
that we've had to reconsider our pact of indifference—
not in fear of their biting our new girl:
she just hasn't learned yet
to discern all the objects of her world, to live and let live,
and not devour each smaller thing within her grasp.

The Second Law of Thermodynamics

"I recall when I was in my prime
I could be happy without cause for joy."
—T'ao Ch'ien

We turn off the television and then all of the lights but one,
the large white globe which we dim down low.
I tell her that we should pick up her toys
and we together fill up a large carton
with books and stuffed animals which have today caught her eye.
The deadbolt on our apartment door is next locked
and we switch on the nitelite in the bathroom near her door.
In her room her mother stands waiting
holding her favorite blanket and a change of clothes.
I kiss her on the cheek and say goodnight
and return to the living room and the rest of the toys.
I find a hand puppet stuck under an ottoman
and there are blocks large and small
still scattered about by the credenza on the floor.
I can hear my wife singing a lullaby to her
as I lie on my stomach reaching under the coffee table for a car.
And somehow I am reminded of a fact I once learned,
of a law from my chemistry class that concludes
that everything will turn to chaos after a while.
I smile to myself as I survey the room.
That day will come soon I already know;
the harbinger is here, our Princess of Anarchy.

This Daughter

It took millions of years
to arrange this just so

—her wide, trusting eyes and pug nose,
the fat, pinkish cheeks

and a forehead large and round,
all put together in familiar fashion,

a cute semblance of me,
bringing back memories

of my own innocence and dreams,
all for one purpose,

for this tug in my heart,
this urge to protect

and to nurture along
until that time when her turn will come

to continue our likeness here
on the face of this earth.

Resemblances

As her head came out
our doctor winked: red hair!

But really there was no denying it —
I was the father.
My wife's first glance
and a voice of shock and mild disappointment:
she looks like you.

And that's what I wisecrack to all my friends
who comment on how cute she is:
resembles her father, right?

It's in the eyes, I think;
like when she smiles
they crinkle like my mother's used to.
That's what I told my aunties last week.
I also said that when she cries
her face and mouth turn oval
reminding me of my father.

That broke them up.
It's an inside joke with our family.
Their brother, though, in his own way
must have loved me
                    just as much.

We Visit My Eldest Brother's for Dinner

I show her the room
I used to stay in

now papered over
with shiny flowers.

This weight room
I point out

was once a study.
I lead her over

to the large framed photos
on the credenza:

this is Daddy's daddy,
and Daddy's mommy.

She cocks her head
looking up at me

with squinting eyes
and a smirk

that feigns disbelief.
Daddy was once a baby too,

just as she was,
she nods knowingly.

We grin impishly
over our secret

of this common history
and hand in hand

go back down the stairs
to join the others.

Part Three

Urban Love Songs

after Tzu Yeh

You stop to watch the Mandarin ducks.
The rest of us continue on to the flamingo lagoon.
I would like to ask what attracts you to them.
But my feet keep walking, I don't look back.

*   *   *

From a piece of cloth I cut out a heart.
In the laundromat it is washed and dried.
I can spend whole hours watching it toss and tumble.
I wonder if you feel the same way as I.

*   *   *

I wave as you enter; you take your seat smiling.
This same coffee shop now feels crowded.
We whisper to each other:
all eyes have noticed something's changed.

*   *   *

I've bought a new phone and an answering machine
because I know you will be calling.
Here's the number, which only you will have.
I plan to change the tape every hour on the hour.

*   *   *

Our friends are laughing.
They say we sit so close in your old Buick
it has become second nature for me
to exit on the same side as you.

*   *   *

Pinoccio's back!
Let's relive that night at the drive in
when I whispered that his nose was giving me ideas
and you got into my pants for the first time.

*   *   *

You drop the laundry off going to work.
I bring the bag back when I come home.
Neatly folded, your underthings are left on the bed
—I wish to respect certain cabinets as yours.

*   *   *

You shut the window rushing to your covers
complaining of the cold night.
I need fresh air, but am willing to compromise.
Let's just pull up the sash halfway, okay?

*   *   *

We hunt for photos in my parents' storeroom.
Look how young I was and full of dreams.
On the way out you brush against a cobweb.
Your flailing arms make me afraid.

*   *   *

A firetruck screams through my heart.
Douse the flames! Douse the flames!
I awake to find my pillow soaked with sweat.
For a moment I thought it was my tears.

*   *   *

You've stacked your boxes neatly by the door.
I find atop one Chinese poems I had bought for us.

Quietly I take the book out.
I resolve to tell you this after you have moved.

*   *   *

For my clogged sink I called a plumber.
When my cat got ill I took her to the vet.
My heart is broken
—I will not ask you to come to mend me.

*   *   *

Last night you made me so mad.
I've resolved never ever to speak to you again.
I regret having to put my foot down so.
I'm sending you a telegram to let you know.

*   *   *

One friend I know cut her hair short.
Another shaved his beard without regrets.
I would walk this city naked and bald
if ever I thought I could be free of you.

*   *   *

After you, I took up jogging.
I wore through my running shoes in no time.
One night I chucked them down into the trash chute.
See how trim I am these days!

*   *   *

Once I bought a single chrysanthemum on a stem.
We watched it blossom, red and full.
Those times now bring a smile to me
finding its brown petals as I sweep the floor.

What Sweet Dream

Waking up at four a.m.
to my shorts
more sticky than wet
I am not embarrassed
to tell you this
even if by implication
it means somehow
we've not been
getting enough of it
after so many years
of our marriage.
I'm only peeved
that I've grown so old
not being able
as before
to recall what sweet dream
it was this time
that I had with you.

Expounding the Doubtful Points

"A good poem excites our admiration
Together we expound the doubtful points."
—T'ao Ch'ien

There are nights when I can't fall asleep
and I stay out in the living room
watching movies on cable
with the volume turned down low
so as not to wake you.
And at other times I'm so beat
that I hit the sack before you come home
from your evening T'ai Chi class
foregoing even any of our goodnight exchanges.
And then once in a while
we wind up in bed together
reading our respective books or newspapers
like the time I was so down
because of all of the razzle dazzle
in the poetry I was reading.
It was like what John once pointed out
that some people get so caught up
in their fancy dribbling
they forget to put the ball
up into the basket.
And I guess to perk me up
I pulled out one of my favorites,
Chaves' book on Mei Yao-ch'en,
which describes Mei's dictum
of the "even and bland"
and how he had championed
writing about the everyday world
without fanfare, just simply and directly
—so different from the usual bombardment
of ornate images and personal allusions
like of going on a trip
trying to jam a single suitcase with clothes

for every season, every conceivable occasion.
At least that's my personal taste
just like Eric's ice cream poetics
that maybe it's just that some people
prefer chocolate and others vanilla.
In Mei's time it seemed
a lot of people were into tall, layered parfaits
with dollops of whipped cream
and chopped nuts sprinkled on top
and a red cherry to boot
—but not too much ice cream
when you came right down to it.
They were called the Hsi K'un School
alluding to a supposed hidden treasure of books
in the K'un Lun Mountains in the West.
And I wanted to tell you
about what I was reading
because I figured you might be interested
having majored in Chinese literature
and taught it for nine years and all.
I knew you had read a little of Mei,
more though his famous friends,
Ou-yang Hsiu and Su Shih.
So I asked if you had ever heard
of the Hsi K'un, but using Cantonese,
guessing at how to actually pronounce the term.
I knew that the first word meant "West"
and so was pronounced *Sài*.
But the "K'un" I didn't have
the foggiest idea of,
the name coming out like *Kwán* maybe.
I suspect you must have said to yourself
well here we go again
pointing out to me that what I just said
sounded more like "bacteria."
And so I tried other variations

like "Saigon" or worse
making you more and more exasperated
until I hit on the right word and inflection
or at least I think you imagined I did
for all of a sudden you blurted out
the *Sài Kwān Tái* I was trying to say.
It was like I had dredged up
from your Sung dynasty lit class
some foul unspeakable name
as you sat up as if taken aback.
And then I explained that Mei, my hero,
didn't like those guys and their style.
It was amazing—
you gave such a sigh of relief
and told me gruffly
you never liked them either
but that when I first mentioned that name
you thought that I did
and were about ready to divorce me.
And then we both laughed
at each other and ourselves
for this momentary misunderstanding
and our happy ending.
It's that we discovered, once again,
that even as we lead our separate lives
we can both still enjoy
ice cream moments such as this
filled with our common love
like a cone of our favorite vanilla
that Häagen-Dazs makes
laced now with orange swirls.

Part Four

At a Chinaman's Grave

"Kingston, too, looked critically at it
['Chinaman'] as not being meaningful for her...
She said she even tried 'Chinaperson' and 'Chinawoman'
and found they didn't work either, the first sounding
'terrible' and the second being inaccurate."
—*The Honolulu Advertiser,* July 22, 1978

My grandmother's
brother here
died all alone, wife
and children back
in the village. He
answered to
"Chinaman" like all
the others
of our race back then.
The Demons hired
only lonely
men, not their
sweethearts,
*tai po*s, baby
daughters. They laid
ties, cut cane, but
could not
proliferate. They took
on woman's
work, by default,
washing shirts,
frying eggs and sausages.
Granduncle cooked.
From what he earned
he sent
money home,
gambled perhaps, maybe hid
some away—all for
one purpose. Those old men:
they lived

their whole
lives with souls
somewhere else, their hearts
burdened of
hopes, waiting to
be reunited.
Some succeeded
and we
are the fruits of those
reunions. Some
did not,
and they are
now forgotten, but for
these tombstones,
by the rest.

The Return of Charlie Chan

after a Frank O'Hara poem

I've called up Eric this afternoon
to inform him that as usual several in our study group
have as yet to pick up their xeroxed sets,
even though the meeting's only three days away.
While listening to him, I notice
my stomach feeling all warm and contented inside
because of the Curry Chicken on Rice
I had at Kowloon Restaurant for lunch today.
After I hang up, I go to the kitchen
to unload the dishwasher
and run the disposal a couple of times,
and my wife who's also in the kitchen
asks me about Laurence Yep whom we've never met
but is coming to stay with us for a week.
She wants to know what kind of breakfast he eats
so she can go out to buy some.
But I don't know, and say so,
and finish off the small remainder
of a can of Coke I find in the icebox.
I go to my desk to work on stuffing our *leih sih*
because it's Chinese New Year
and because we always pass out red envelopes
with Susan B. Anthony dollars to kids of our friends.
But after looking around a while,
I can't seem to find the coins
—which I decide I've left down at the office.
So I go back to the living room
where the *Star-Bulletin*'s laid out on the floor
and I turn straight to the Amusements page
and immediately see the ad for your new movie
and your face which I stare at
and stare at for a full two minutes.
I remember more out of sadness than rage
the mincing way you walk and your fortune cookie talk

and your pressed white suit with matching hat.
You are still the most famous Chinaman in all America
and you will never let us forget it.

Local Sensibilities

inspired by Frank Chin

When I see a pineapple,
I do not think of an exotic fruit sliced in rings
        to be served with ham,
more the summer jobs at the cannery
        driving a forklift or packing wedges on the line.

When I hear the name "Duke,"
I envision someone other than that movie cowboy,
        gravel-voiced, a true grit idol of the late night set;
instead I see a white-haired surfer by his long board,
        palms so large, flashing smiles along the beach.

When I think of a man-of-war,
it is not the name of a Triple Crown horse
        pacing a stud farm that comes to mind first;
rather I picture the Portuguese kind
        whose stings must be salved by rubbing sand.

When I use the word "packages,"
it is usually not a reference to the parcels
        waiting for me at the post office,
rather the paper sacks I get
        from the supermarket to lug my groceries home.

When I read the term "Jap,"
the image of a kamikaze pilot now turned to Sony exports
        is not what I see;
mainly it is the Sand Island roundup and those old men
        who still wince long after the 442nd has marched back.

When I think of Hawaii,
I do not fancy myself lolling under palm trees,
        a backdrop of verdant cliffs, caressed by a balmy breeze;
instead I give thanks for classmates and our family graves,
        this unique universe that we have called our home.

Terms of Assimilation

You must become
an ass

      or worse:
the mule, that
cross between a male donkey
and a mare,

         is
perforce sterile.

Minority Poem

Why
we're just as American
as apple pie—
that is, if you count
the leftover peelings
lying on the kitchen counter
which the cook has forgotten about
or doesn't know
quite what to do with
except hope that the maid
when she cleans off the chopping block
will chuck them away
into a garbage can she'll take out
on leaving for the night.

Upon Hearing about
the 1971 Fourth Coming of Charlie Chan

So sorry,
but I never heard of it
till now. I know what I would do
though.
       Late at night
I'd steal a ladder, climb all the way
up to the marquee
of Grauman's Chinese Theatre.
During the next morning I'd gorge
myself full of bananas,
waiting.
       I'd watch
as little by little the crowd
would form, then the sudden
applause—
       Ross Martin in his tuxedo
with no shoes, coming down
the sidewalk to be
cemented.
       Just as he passes
below me, I'd whip out
my Yellow Peril
to drench him.
       You see, I know
from experience: no matter
how many bananas
I eat, my piss
always keeps coming out yellow.

Translations

1

Ghosts: they conjure
up childhood
scenes—me running around in
old bedsheets, reading
about Caspar
next to a comic
rack, marvelling at
the trick
camerawork for Cosmo G. Topper.

Gwái: I am older now,
sometimes catch previews
to those Shaw Brothers horror
films, at the
library research ancient
rites of exorcism for
the baneful
who brought pestilence and
drought. There are also,
I have
learned, Old Demons who wear
white skin
and make believe
they behave
like men.

2

The Chinaman gave
the Demon what
the former thought
the latter thought
were things
Chinese: a comedy

of errors,
part fawning, part
deception and contempt.
There is no
word for
fortune cookie in Cantonese.

3

Tòhng Yàhn Gāai was what
we once called
where we
lived: "China-People-
Street." Later, we mimicked
Demon talk
and wrote down only
Wàh Fauh—"China-Town."
The difference
is obvious: the people
disappeared.

Going Home

Ngóh m̀h sīk góng tòhng wá—
besides the usual menu words,
the only phrase I really know,
I say it loudly,
but he is not listening.
He keeps on talking with his smile,
staring, it would seem, past me
into the night without a moon.

He's lost, presumably.
But I don't know what he's saying.
He is an old man, wearing a hat,
and the kind of overcoat
my father wears:
the super-padded shoulders.
His nostrils trickle with wet drops,
which he does not care to wipe away.

Ngóh m̀h sīk góng tòhng wá—
I try again, to no avail.
I try in English: what street?
and think of taking out
some paper and a pen.
                           Just then,
two young fellows approach us
carrying a chair; one look
and I can tell
that *they* will oblige him.
I sigh, and point them out,
and hastily cross the street,
escaping. Once on the other side,
I glimpse around, and catch
their gestures from afar,
still able to hear those familiar,
yet no less incomprehensible sounds.

I head home, and visualize
this old man with his small beady eyes
and the two glistening lines
below them, vertical,
like make-up for some clown.
Out loud, I wonder:
but Chinamen aren't supposed to cry.

Riding the North Point Ferry

Wrinkles: like
valleys etched by glaciers
lumbering coarse
and deliberate, random
traces pointing to
that vast, dark sea. The skin
is an ochre
of old corn, with
splotches of
burnt embers from a summer
of mountain fires.
The brown
from a lifetime of tea or
tobacco or both
has stained her
uneven teeth. Ears and nose
are small, pudgy,
and on each
lobe a little knob of gold
tacked on.
She sits with one
leg raised, tucked
into her body, the heel
supported by
the seat, her arm
resting on her
knee—unladylike to be
sure, though
in her black garments
a relaxed pose. I glance at
her eyes, mottled
now with a chicken fat-
yellow in the
pupils, gazing out at the harbor,
the neon lights beckoning
from the Kowloon
shore.

          Where
was I prepared for this
face? Not
from the land of
my birth, with our museums,
glass cases filled
with the porcelain of ancient
dynasties, restaurateurs (cheeks
of cupidity)
proffering hot
and sour delights, our bookstores
extolling Shangri-las in
paperback—all to deny
our scrutable
lives. We believe
that somewhere in the world our
exotica is real. Images
of all fairy tale
maidens: clear-eyed yet
coy, hair pure
as silk, skin like jade,
the small hands so clever and
refined—and when
held in my own, how
warm, yielding to the touch!
They are
fiction: like the wind-blown
waves across this
ferry's bow, an inconstant
surface of
reflection, glittering, oblivious
to the swollen
depths below.

          I know
that outward appearances are
no judge for
virtue within. And
even this old

woman, combing her loosed
hair at dawn,
must sometimes wonder
at that mirrored form, peering
from those eyes. Does
she recognize
that dark glow as
her own? We meet so many
dreams, so many tales
of woe. Which
ones are true? Which ones
our alibis? So hard to
choose.

      My grandparents
I recall sailed by
sea to settle in
that place we now call home.
I have crossed that
ocean too, flying this time
with the sun,
searching for a vision
for my own. The deck rocks gently.
By chance I find
myself beside this woman
on this crowded
boat: she is
for me reason enough to
have come here.

To the Old Masters

"They may have left behind an honored name
but it cost a lifetime of deprivation."
— T'ao Ch'ien

I have no wife,
much less a son, to lament over
when he has died
in his infancy. I have never
seen a peach
blossom in the bud,
nor stood beneath
the Red Cliffs awed by
their towering history. Alcohol
tastes bitter
to me; I have always shunned
such classic delights.
Few friends
of mine write
poems—even letters are hard to
compose: how can we
swap our sentiments? Poring
over your lyrics,
the translations at my
side, I worry about how
muddle-headed my past innocence
has made me. This
is my only
claim to sorrow. Whatever
glimpses I have
caught of the vision within
your words must be due to
your daring: as
the moon on this night
illumines to the far reaches
of my room,
beaming through a window

78

cluttered now with
clothes, drying in the breeze.

Quarry Bay, 1974

Taking Her to the Open Market

Scales glisten;
pink whiskers jut out.
Some are the color
of mud, others
recall the embroidery
of coats placed
on babes one month old.
Fat, round, small:
they lay on the crushed
ice, stall after stall.

"Look at the fresh fish!"
I exclaim, eager to impress
on her our respect
for the old
ways, and that I know
how to tell the firmness
a poached flesh will have
by the bulging
of its eyes, the blood
in the gills.

"They are dead,"
she replies. Taken aback,
I see
through her Hong Kong eyes
that fresh
means leaning over
a galvanized pan, eyeing
closely through the running
water at that
cluster of darting
shadows, seeking out the one
swimming most
vigorously: in demonstration
that it

has not yet
passed the point of no return.

"We have,"
I mutter, "killed off
more than germs."

Discovering You Speak Cantonese

Our discourses have been learned:
your roommate's briefs on rent control,
Alinsky and the attorney's role,
the mainland Chinamen's impressions of us Pakes.

While waiting at a reading,
I discover you too
went to Hong Kong to learn Chinese.
My immigrant wife eager to test you out
switches us out of English.

Your tones are funny;
you sometimes stop
searching for a forgotten phrase.

I catch myself talking slower,
conscious that I must not discourage
or put you down.

An eerie feeling comes over me.
Our relationship, once equal,
borders on the awkward: paternalistic airs.

I know now
how my wife feels talking to me.

My Brother Returns

"When we parted you were unmarried.
Now you have a row of boys and girls.
They smile at this old friend of their father's
and ask me from where have I come."
—Tu Fu

The village is small;
the driver does not know how to find it.

Peasant girls on bicycles
point to a cluster of buildings
nestled in the embrace of a distant hill.

The bumpy dirt road curves, then narrows
—their van must stop.

On foot they make their way past sunken ricefields.
With the sky overcast
the mainland winter hugs their parkas.

My brother asks if anyone recalls our grandfather
who left for Hawaii one hundred years before.

An old woman leads them
to a row of stone houses covered with soot and grime.
Pigs and ducks waddle about in the concrete yard.

A crowd surrounds them.
Suddenly a lean, dark-skinned elder rushes forward.

The man claims to be a first cousin of our father
and bears a resemblance to album photos
of our father's brother when he was young.

Out loud the elder recites from the family tree
and my brother picks out his own name in Chinese.

Our new uncle brings out a bundle of letters.
They are still in their envelopes
and were written by our father from after the war.

Separated by decades two families gather for photos.
The sun obliges and comes out beaming.

An Aloha Only I Could Feel

It was hot; there was little time.
We had come from so far away

without the certainty
that we could find him.
He had just returned from the fields

to avoid the noontime heat
and we arrived unannounced.

He was my father's cousin,
of the branch that stayed behind.
I was not the first from our side

to visit him,
and we had corresponded before.

We talked about the usual things,
his crops, the factories
where his sons now worked,

the dead that were our common bond.
Maybe I was tired then,

from all the travelling,
for after a while
I did not know what else to say.

Here was an old man, darkly tanned,
whose whole world,

his daily life, his hopes and fears,
were so unlike mine.
What did he know of how I lived,

my business, all my learning?
And yet suddenly

something welled up in me,
a sense of pride, of being special,
that I belonged to him

and him to me,
that no one else would ever have,

an aloha only I could feel,
because of blood,
and of those dead we talked about

who loved and cared for him
just as they did for me.

But My Smile

It was good. We saw the ricefields,
the brick houses, the duckponds and pigs.

Our relative, a brown and wiry man,
turned out to be very friendly.

He worked his own fields
and his children all had jobs in factories.

Recently he had even built for them
a new two-story house just behind his own.

It was there that we sat and chatted
as if we had known each other for years.

Even our daughter who often gets restless
was somehow well-behaved

as if she also knew
how important the day was for all of us.

At the end we gathered outside
for photographs all around.

As we were saying our goodbyes
I noticed a black pig wandering by.

It stopped in the middle of the courtyard
to piss in front of us without care.

Our daughter laughed out loud
amused and surprised.

We exchanged knowing smiles
but my smile was also for something more.

My grandfather left this village
one hundred years before.

In spite of all that I saw that day
I am grateful that he did.

Grateful Here

1

Emerging from the subway station,
then lost among the orange signs on Nedicks snackbars,
I could smell the thick rice soup and dumplings
I would order in that basement lunchroom
already beckoning me. I thought:
like a salmon returning to its spawning ground
—and, bemused, followed my Chinese nose.

2

Early one Sunday morning each spring,
our family would visit my grandparents' graves,
offering gifts of tea and suckling pig,
burning colored paper, incense, and loud firecrackers.
Later, my mother would take me to church.
I sang in the choir and would carry, that day,
fragile lilies to the altar of my risen Lord.

3

When walking with a Caucasian girl,
holding hands, I would pass by teenage hangouts,
overhearing insults. They would always pick on the girl,
as though she were a lesbian.
Separately, I guess, we would pretend
not to have noticed—avoiding embarrassment
for the other, tightening our grips.

4

Observing two gay Negroes, powdered gray,
and strutting regally on their high-heeled boots,
I followed them half-enviously with my eyes,
understanding, for the first time, that dark allure

of nighttime caresses. I was in rural Pennsylvania,
and found housewives at the grocer's brought their children
with small, craning necks to whisper about me.

5

After a sit-in at the Pentagon,
the arresting marshall misspelt my name.
Actually, though, I know I should feel grateful here.
In fact, just last week on the radio, I heard
that the Red Guards had broken the wrists
of a most promising young pianist. Among other things,
he had journeyed to the West to play Beéthoven and Brahms.

Juk

was what I used to eat
a lot of—like everyday
I'd cross the street to Hong Wah's
for a take-out. On seeing me
the owner by the register
would try to outguess me.
Waaht Gāi Jūk, she'd bellow
in a knowing way,
as if it were my name.

It was a game we played.
Depending on my whim
I'd simply nod my head, assenting,
or correct her, smiling:
Fó Ngáap—to which she'd call
the order out again,
so that the waiter down the aisle
could write it for the kitchen.

Later, if she got a chance,
she'd go back personally.
You could see her through the open door:
first, with a ladle scooping
the soup, a light sprinkle
of scallions, and then the quick plop
of a handful of duck, chopped
in chunks, covered
I knew with lots of skin.

She would fill out a few orders
like this: soup
in the red containers, the dishes
of rice and of noodles
into white boxes. In turn,
they would all be dropped
into bags, which she'd carry

—maybe three to an arm—
as she rushed, waddling,
up to the front.
                    Sometimes,
I wondered if the hectic pace
would kill her in a year.
At other times I felt:
she's probably now a millionaire.
No one has made as good
a juk since then. I hope it tasted
as good to her
                    as it did to me.

Chinese New Year

The Senator has sent us soup and oranges;
we give them to the old men
who push each other out of line.

For dinner I order monk's food on rice.
The owner rings up a dollar thirty-three
and gives me back a quarter.

In the basement of a Catholic church
I watch a comedy in Cantonese
—I'm beginning to understand a little.

Listening to the firecrackers on Mott Street,
I remember that for others this is Tet,
and that today their war is not yet over.

Chinatown Games

inspired by Fung Shiu-Ying's
Chinese Children's Games (ARTS, Inc.,
New York City, 1972)

1. Choosing Sides

Little girls
on the sidewalk
chanting in a circle
an even number of them
each offering
a hand outstretched
some palms up
some down.
When by chance
an equal number
show up as down
they gather their teams
ready to play
no hint of ability
just the fun of the game.

2. Sugar Stuck Beans

An even number of kids:
one of them It.
Safety is found
in sticking together—
a pair of beans.
The It can tag you
only if you're alone.
The little ones scream
weave about parked cars
arms locked.
Some sacrifice security
gladly breaking a pair

to distract the It
saving another
dodging all by himself.

3. Hawk Grabbing Chicks

Arms waving
the mother hen
holds her ground
in front of the hawk
her children undulating
in a single line
behind her.
The hawk must go around
to snatch any stray
who might let go
as the hen angles
towards the hydrant
her noisy brood
hands to waist clinging on
for dear life.

Tradition

The mother squats
her breast
pressed against
the small back
and neck
her arms
in a cradle
hooking the knees
up and out
dangling
the little bare ass
over the gutter
just so
ready
for the stream
of pee
to carry the curb

T-Bone Steak

The Chinese cut their meat before
sautéing with
vegetables cut up
the same
way, deeming those individual
portions of steak,
served American-
style, extravagant, dull,
unsociable,
and requiring too
much effort with the knife
while eating.

My father on occasion
brought home
one T-bone. *Máang fó, nyùhn
yàuh,* he cautioned:
heat
the skillet first,
the oil you pour just
before you lay
the steak on.
Delegated, I eased the full
slab on with wooden
chopsticks (forks and
other metal
objects puncture). The black
cast iron
splattered oil. My mother
usually told me to
put on
my shirt.
I lowered the
flame, and
every so often nudged
at the recessed

areas near the bone against
the pan's flat
surface. We
liked our
meat medium-rare, five
minutes to a
side at
most. At the chopping
block, I sliced off long
chunks, a half inch
thick, quickly
serving them on a platter ready
to eat, among
our other
sung, before the blood
oozed out completely.

No, it was not
Chinese, much less
American, that pink piece
sitting in my rice
bowl. It was,
simply, how our family
ate, and I
for one am grateful for
the difference.

A Moon Festival Picnic at Kahala Beach Park

"But why is it always full
just when people are parted?"
—Su Tung P'o

I am sitting on a bench near the beach
with Rolanse and Irene
who like my wife are from Hong Kong.
And each of us has our one kid
on our respective laps
and we are all reciting
a Cantonese nursery rhyme
that starts off celebrating
the brightness of the moon.
And it's just gotten dark and cool
with the full moon
rising off the water from the east,
lemon-hued, and fat and sassy,
like the cheerful face of a child
playing peek-a-boo among the clouds.
And I am content
to just sit and relax on this bench
having just stuffed myself
with fresh clams from Tamashiro's
and some barbeque chicken
and a lot of potato salad.
And I recall from my experience
living in Hong Kong
that each year on this eighth moon
families always gathered together
for a special dinner
—like my wife's folks
who without fail
served a whole chicken and shrimp
and a soup made from pork and lotus root.
And even now my wife reminisces
about how her father

always made a big deal
about having to buy
a certain kind of vegetarian mooncake
only made at this time of the year.
And then I begin to think
about these sentiments
and how they've been
in this culture of ours for generations.
It reminds me of something
that my wife once did—suddenly—
when we were on a date one night
near the Star Ferry
walking outdoors under the moon.
She recited for me from memory
a poem by Tu Fu, in exile,
wanting to be with his family
on this same festival night.
He had looked up at the moon
and found solace that his brothers too,
though far away,
were somehow viewing
his same moon at the same time.
It is as if even then
custom had already been imprinted
within our race
—the desire of families
to be with each other
coursing through our blood
at this moon's first waxing.
And I think of asking Rolanse and Irene
about their own families
and about what family traditions
they would be observing
in Hong Kong right about now.
But maybe it's because before dinner
I was listening to Sam

who programs the computer
for the Planetarium's show
talk about the moon
and how it spins around the earth
in the same clockwise direction
as our planet's own rotation.
For it suddenly dawns on me
that this levitating ball in the sky,
growing paler and smaller
as we sit here,
is not yet in the heavens over Hong Kong
or for that matter
over anywhere in all of China,
separated as we are
by some half an ocean
following in the flightpath of the moon.
In fact because of the dateline
they've already celebrated
this festival our time yesterday.
It's just one more difference
to our overseas Chinese lives, I decide,
thinking now of the moon's path
as some discarded umbilical cord
or a lifeline unravelling.
And I look at these three little ones here,
their round heads bobbing up and down
in time to our chanting,
to a cadence even now
they do not hear in their preschools.
Each of them was born here
in this new land,
young settlers for whom
the changes of the moon
will merely mean a cold astronomy,
for whom a grandparent
will just bring to mind

a small voice across a long distance line.
And I wonder what new traditions
will be passed down
to their own children
years from now on this night.
And as they look out
at the expanse of this dark ocean
I can see their wide open eyes
sparkling from the brilliance in the sky
like the candied squash and apricots
that we will pass out later.
It is from the excitement of the hour,
of all of us together,
that fills their voices,
a sense of a new family,
of these children and their parents
and their parents' friends.
I hold on to my daughter tightly
resolving next year to return
with her and with these others
for another picnic by this beach
to marvel once again
at this same full-flowering of the moon.

On the First Proper Sunday of Ching Ming

We arrive at seven
    when the cemetery unlocks its long chain;
    as usual, others have shown up even earlier.

Lugging boxes of food through the rows of graves
    I remember as a child being scolded:
    never step on someone else's mound.

We lay out our dishes systematically.
    There are seven ancestors to do
    and we want to beat the crowds arriving later.

Here and there I see families tending to their own.
    A rush comes over me: we are like them.
    I feel proud, grateful for being Chinese.

Harvest Festival Time

Those hard-scrabble folk in broad-brimmed
hats, blunderbusses
warm, handling fat
buckles, many women with dour, pious
faces, sitting
on benches, their backs
to the Old Country: spread before
them are pumpkin
pies, hot-
buttered corn
on the cob, all manner of
squash, stuffing and sliced turkey.
They wait
for the gaunt, brown
men—fellow colonists from across
another sea—who
one by
one straggle in. Some
bring loud
wives, beloved children.
They wear long gowns, pantaloons and
tunics of cotton
and silk, carrying to
the tables tall
pots of
rice gruel, white tripe, assorted
moon cake. A goose
would be juicier, a Chinaman
winks. Puritans smirk,
nodding to the
viscera floating in the gruel. We
eat our own food,
all
agree. They manage smiles,
and dig in.

Thanksgiving, 1979

Chinese Hot Pot

My dream of America
is like *dá bìn lòuh*
with people of all persuasions and tastes
sitting down around a common pot
chopsticks and basket scoops here and there
some cooking squid and others beef
some tofu or watercress
all in one broth
like a stew that really isn't
as each one chooses what he wishes to eat
only that the pot and fire are shared
along with the good company
and the sweet soup
spooned out at the end of the meal.

Special Dedications

"To a Classmate Just Dead" for Laurence Leavitt
"She Made Quite Sure of That" for a classmate who's concerned about how her
    children will react
"This Intimacy" for Gary
"The Return of Charlie Chan" for Hal Lum, 1981
"Terms of Assimilation" for Talk Story Conference, June 21, 1978
"Minority Poem" for George Lee
"Upon Hearing about the 1971 Fourth Coming of Charlie Chan" for Frankie
"Translations" for Jeffery Paul Chan in appreciation of his letter to the editor,
    New York Review of Books, April 28, 1977
"Discovering You Speak Cantonese" for David M. Louie, Esq.
"T-Bone Steak" for Ben Tong
"Harvest Festival Time" for Chiye Mori, Editor, *Manzanar Free Press*